# Fall Fun from A-Z!

## LETTER & NUMBER RECOGNITION

### LETTER SOUNDS    COUNTING

### MATCHING and More!

## Mary Mack Prince

Welcome to *Ms. Mary Mack Publishing*! We are glad you're here! This book is a fun way to discuss things we might see and do during the fall season while practicing letters, numbers, and colors. See how many things in the book you find at school. How many things do you have at your house? Look outside and see how many things you can find from the book. Have fun learning and sharing what you learn!

# A a

**A**pple Se**a**son

# B b

**B**oy & **B**ook

# C c

Crayons

# D d

**D**eer

# E e

**E**rasers

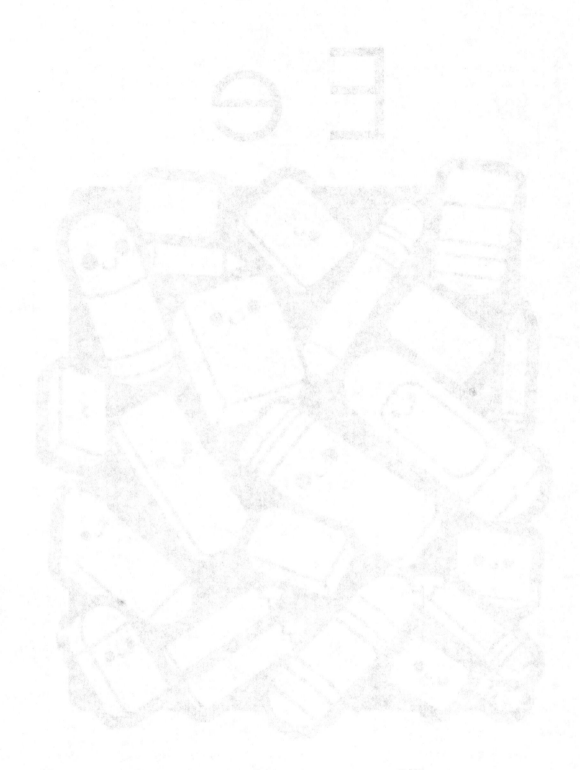

# F f

**F**riends

# G g

**G**iving Thanks

# H h

**H**orse eating **h**ay

# I i

Inside

# J j

**J**ack-o-lantern

# K k

# Karate

K k

karate

# L l

Leaves

# M m

**M**oon

# N n

# Notebook

Owl

# P p

**P**um**p**kin

# Q q

# Quilt

# R r

**R**ake

# S s

# Scarecrow

# Your feedback is greatly appreciated!

It's through your feedback, support and reviews that we're able to create the best books possible and serve more people. We would be extremely grateful if you could take just 60 seconds to kindly leave an honest review of the book on Amazon. Please share your feedback and thoughts for others to see. To do so, simply find the book on Amazon's website ( https://a.co/d/93ZCSJj ) and locate the section to leave a review. Select a star rating and write a couple of sentences.

That's it! Thank you so much for your support.

## Review this product

Share your thoughts with other customers

Write a customer review

# T t

# Trick-or-Treat!

# U u

**U**mbrella

# V v

**V**egetables

# W w

**W**indy **W**eather!

# X x

**X** marks the spot!

# Y y

**Y**ou! Draw **y**ourself smiling!

# Z z

# Zipper

# Zz

Zipper

# Count and Color

Have fun counting and coloring all the things you see!

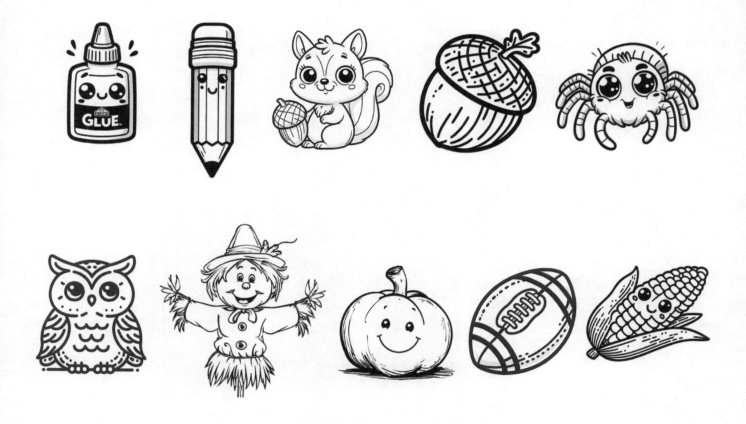

# 1

# One

1

One

# 2

**Two**

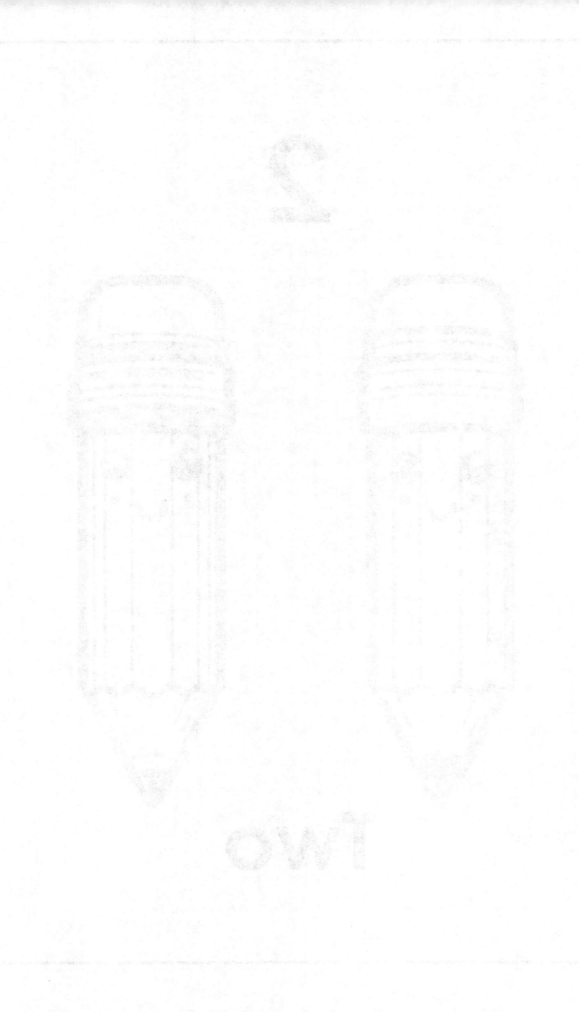

2

two

# 3

# Three

# 4

# Four

# 5

# Five

# 6

# Six

# 7

Seven

**8**

# Eight

# 9

# Nine

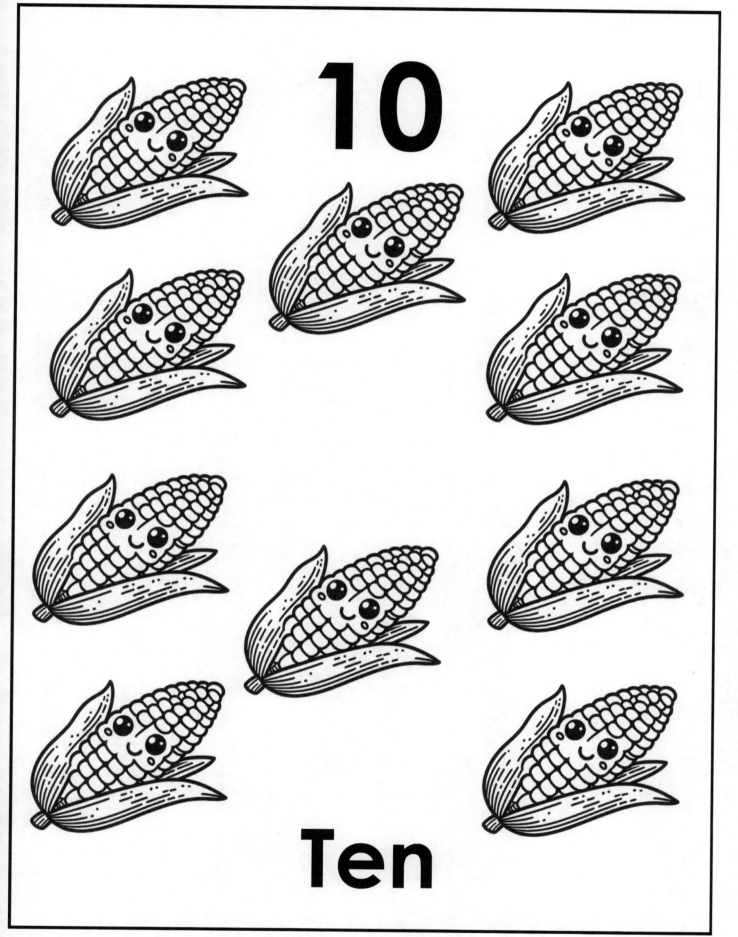

10

Ten

Circle who might live in a tree.
Mark an "X" if they would not.

Circle who might live in a tree.
mark an "X" if they would not.

# Match and color the pictures.

# Color each crayon.

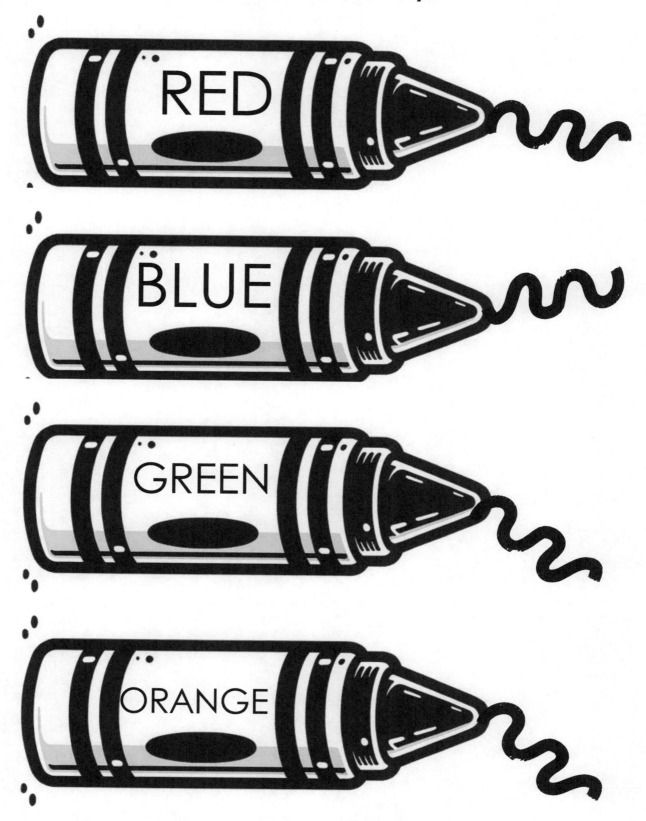

RED

BLUE

GREEN

ORANGE

# Draw what you love!

# Trace the dots to connect the pictures.

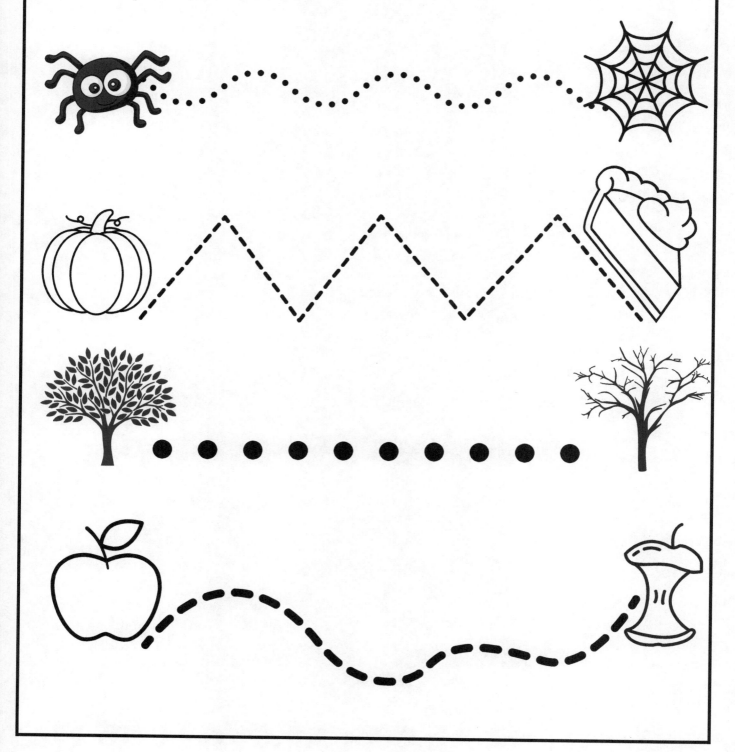

Trace the dots to connect
the pictures.

# Add rain and light up the clouds with lightning!

Who lives in the house? Is the sun shining or is it cloudy?

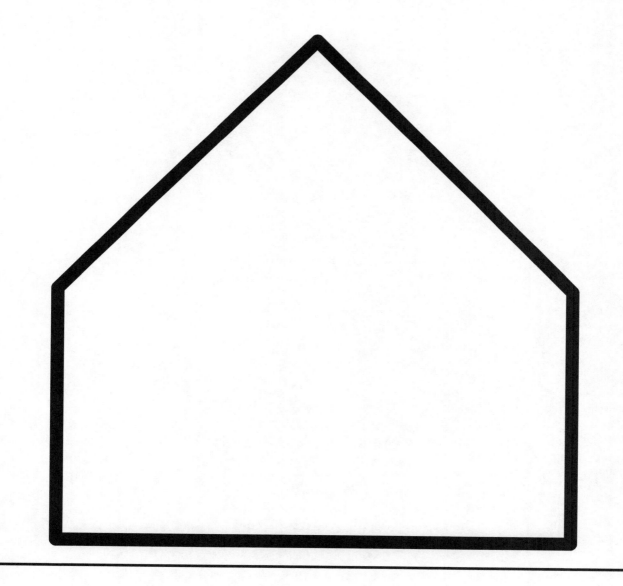

# Draw Emotions on the Pumpkins.

Happy

Sad

Scared

Mad

Sad

Mad

# Fun Chat Prompts for the Whole Family!

Take turns letting everyone share their answers.

1. Where would you land if you were a fall leaf in the wind?

2. How many pumpkins could you carry at the same time?

3. Would you have a squirrel for a pet?

4. How many seeds do you think are inside of a pumpkin?

5. What do you love about school?

6. If your backpack could talk, what would it say?

7. What is your favorite thing to eat for lunch on a school day?

8. Have you ever jumped into a pile of fall leaves?

9. What is your favorite kind of weather?

10. Would you have a spider for a pet?

Made in United States
Troutdale, OR
10/16/2024

23836842R00058